The
McCormick

Cookbook

SMITHMARK

This edition published in 1991 by Ottenheimer Publishers, Inc. for
SMITHMARK Publishers Inc., 112 Madison Avenue, New York, NY 10016.

SMITHMARK books are available for bulk purchase, for sales promotion and
premium use. For details write or telephone the Manager of Special Sales,
SMITHMARK Publishers Inc., 112 Madison Avenue, New York, NY 10016.
(212) 532-6600.

Contents

Introduction

The McCormick Cookbook offers "a whole world of good tastes." A delicious variety of recipes developed and tested in the McCormick/Schilling Culinary Center will spice up your family's eating habits. Delectable dishes contain a variety of McCormick spices, seasonings, and flavorings.

McCormick & Company, Inc. has a long and illustrious history in the food industry. In September 1889, Willoughby M. McCormick first began making fruit syrups in a basement in downtown Baltimore. From there, McCormick grew to become the world's largest producer of spices, seasonings, and flavorings. In addition, McCormick has been an innovator in introducing gourmet spices, convenience products, and easy-to-use containers. You'll find that aromatic and flavorful McCormick products make all meals special.

Appetizers and Soups

Oysters Rockefeller   *6 to 8 servings*

¾ cup butter
1 (10-ounce) package frozen chopped
   spinach, thawed and drained
1 tablespoon McCormick® Instant
   Minced Onion
1 teaspoon McCormick Parsley Flakes
½ teaspoon McCormick Chervil Leaves
⅛ teaspoon McCormick Tarragon
   Leaves
½ teaspoon McCormick Bon Appétit®

⅛ teaspoon McCormick Ground Red
   Pepper
⅛ teaspoon McCormick Ground White
   Pepper
Dash McCormick Instant Garlic
   Powder
2 tablespoons fine dry, unseasoned
   bread crumbs
Rock salt
24 oysters on the half shell
Hollandaise Sauce (recipe below)

Melt butter in saucepan. Add spinach, minced onion, parsley flakes, chervil, tarragon, Bon Appétit, red and white peppers, and garlic powder to butter. Simmer mixture 15 minutes. Remove from heat. Add bread crumbs. Preheat broiler. Spread layer of rock salt in shallow baking pan. Arrange oysters on salt. Spread 1 tablespoon of spinach mixture over each oyster. Top each oyster with 1½ teaspoons Hollandaise Sauce. Broil 4 to 5 inches from heat for 4 minutes. Serve immediately.

Hollandaise Sauce   *¾ cup*

1 (1.25-ounce) package McCormick
   Hollandaise Sauce Mix
⅛ teaspoon McCormick Tarragon
   Leaves

⅛ teaspoon McCormick Ground
   Mustard
1 tablespoon olive oil
¾ cup water

Combine all ingredients, except water, in saucepan. Gradually stir in water, mixing well. Cook over medium heat, stirring constantly, until sauce thickens.

Fennel Cheese Spread   *1 cup*

2 (8-ounce) packages cream cheese,
    softened to room temperature
1 teaspoon McCormick *Fennel Seed*
1/4 teaspoon McCormick *Bon Appétit*
1/8 teaspoon McCormick *Ground Savory*
1/8 teaspoon McCormick *Instant Garlic
    Powder*

1/8 teaspoon McCormick *Instant Onion
    Powder*
1/4 teaspoon McCormick *Basil Leaves*
Whole almonds, with skins
Fresh chives
Fresh parsley

Using an electric mixer, beat together cream cheese, fennel, Bon Appétit, savory, garlic and onion powders, and basil. Mix well. Refrigerate mixture 4 hours, or overnight. Mold into pineapple shape with hands. Cover cheese with almonds, starting at the bottom and working up in even rows; push almonds into cheese mixture, pointed end down, overlapping in a shingled manner. Continue until cheese is covered with almonds, leaving a small space in top center. Poke small holes in top of "pineapple" and place tops of fresh chives into cheese. Place small sprigs of parsley around base of chives. Serve at room temperature.

Salmon Mousse   *16 servings*

A great party appetizer that is best prepared the day before.

1/2 cup water
1 envelope unflavored gelatin
2 tablespoons lemon juice
2 tablespoons McCormick *Onion Flakes*
1/2 cup mayonnaise
1 tablespoon prepared horseradish
2 teaspoons McCormick *Dill Weed*

1/2 teaspoon McCormick *Bon Appétit*
1/4 teaspoon McCormick *Paprika*
1 (15- or 16-ounce) can salmon, drained
    and skin removed
1 cup whipping cream
Sliced cucumbers, for garnish

Lightly oil a 4-cup mold. Combine water and gelatin in small saucepan. Let stand 1 minute. Cook over medium heat, stirring constantly, until gelatin dissolves. Pour gelatin into food processor or blender. Add lemon juice and onion flakes. Cover and blend at high speed 10 seconds. Add mayonnaise, horseradish, dill, Bon Appétit, paprika, and salmon; blend 30 seconds. Add whipping cream and blend at high speed until smooth. Pour into prepared mold. Cover and refrigerate until set, at least 2 hours. Unmold onto a serving platter and garnish with sliced cucumbers.

Salmon Mousse

Cheddar-Brie Cheese Soup   *4 servings*

¼ cup butter
¼ cup diced onion
¼ cup diced celery
2 tablespoons flour
2 teaspoons McCormick *Chicken Flavor Base*
1½ cups hot water
1½ cups milk

4 ounces Brie cheese, cubed
8 ounces Cheddar cheese, grated
1 tablespoon Chablis (dry white wine)
¼ teaspoon McCormick *Parsley Flakes*
¼ teaspoon McCormick *Paprika*
¼ teaspoon McCormick *Basil Leaves*
Herbed Croutons (recipe below)

Melt butter in 2-quart saucepan. Add onion and celery; sauté until tender. Stir in flour, using a wire whisk. Cook 3 minutes, stirring constantly. Combine chicken flavor base with water. Slowly add broth and milk to saucepan. Bring to boil, stirring constantly. Lower heat and stir in remaining ingredients. Stir with whisk until cheese melts. Simmer 5 minutes over low heat. Serve hot with Herbed Croutons.

Herbed Croutons   *1½ cups*

½ loaf Italian bread, cut in ½-inch slices
½ cup butter
⅛ teaspoon McCormick *Instant Garlic Powder*

⅛ teaspoon McCormick *Instant Onion Powder*
½ teaspoon McCormick *Basil Leaves*
½ teaspoon McCormick *Marjoram Leaves*

Trim crusts from bread. Cut slices in ½ × 1-inch pieces; set aside. Melt butter in skillet. Add garlic and onion powders, basil, and marjoram. Sauté bread cubes in hot butter mixture, turning to brown all sides. Drain on paper towels.

Note: To vary crouton recipe, substitute ⅛ teaspoon each McCormick freeze-dried Chopped Chives, Tarragon Leaves, and Thyme Leaves in place of other herbs.

Cheddar-Brie Cheese Soup

Tortilla Soup   *7 servings*

This is a meal in one bowl, with a marvelous, rich blend of spice flavors.

1 cup tomato juice
½ cup coarsely chopped celery
½ cup thinly sliced carrots
7 cups hot water
2 tablespoons McCormick Beef Flavor Base
2 whole McCormick Black Peppercorns
1 McCormick Bay Leaf
1 tablespoon McCormick Instant Minced Onion

¼ teaspoon McCormick Instant Garlic Powder
1 (4-ounce) can mild green chillies, drained and cut into strips
2 McCormick Whole Hot Chillies
Meatballs (recipe below)
Tortilla Chips
Monterey Jack cheese, shredded

In large saucepan, combine tomato juice, celery, carrots, hot water, beef flavor base, peppercorns, bay leaf, minced onion, garlic powder, green chillies, and hot chillies. Bring to a boil. Reduce heat and simmer 25 minutes. Remove peppercorns, bay leaf, and hot chillies. To serve soup, place a few meatballs in soup plate. Ladle broth over meatballs. Add a few tortilla chips and sprinkle with shredded cheese.

Meatballs   *About 21 meatballs*

1 tablespoon McCormick Instant Minced Onion
¼ cup fine dry, unseasoned bread crumbs
¼ cup milk
1 egg, beaten
½ pound ground beef
½ pound ground pork
½ cup chopped blanched almonds

⅛ teaspoon McCormick Ground Black Pepper
⅛ teaspoon McCormick Ground Oregano
⅛ teaspoon McCormick Ground Cumin
1 teaspoon McCormick Chervil Leaves
½ teaspoon McCormick Shredded Green Onion
¾ teaspoon McCormick Bon Appétit
1 tablespoon peanut oil

Mix all ingredients, except oil, together in large bowl. Shape in 1¼-inch meatballs. Heat oil in large skillet. Cook meatballs 5 minutes, turning to brown on all sides. Add a small amount more oil if necessary.

Popcorn Soup   *8 servings*

Intrigue your guests with this variation on traditional cream of chicken soup.

1 (2½- to 3-pound) whole broiler-fryer chicken
2 teaspoons McCormick *Parsley Flakes*
6 cups water
1 McCormick *Bay Leaf*
¼ teaspoon McCormick *Thyme Leaves*
2 teaspoons McCormick *Instant Minced Onion*

6 tablespoons butter
6 tablespoons flour
2 cups half-and-half or light cream
1½ teaspoons McCormick *Bon Appétit*
1 tablespoon Chicken Flavor Base
¼ teaspoon McCormick *Ground White Pepper*
½ cup popcorn, popped

Wash chicken. Place in Dutch oven or large stockpot. Add 1 teaspoon parsley flakes, water, bay leaf, thyme, and minced onion. Bring to a boil. Reduce heat, cover, and simmer 35 to 40 minutes, or until chicken is tender. Remove chicken from stock and cool. Strain and reserve 4 cups stock. Remove meat from bones and cut in ½-inch cubes. Melt butter over low heat in Dutch oven or 4-quart pot. Gradually add flour, stirring constantly until smooth. Cook over medium heat until bubbly. Gradually add reserved, strained chicken stock, stirring constantly. Add cream, Bon Appétit, chicken flavor base, white pepper, and remaining parsley flakes. Cook, stirring constantly, over medium heat until mixture begins to boil. Reduce heat and simmer 1 minute. Add chicken. Cook over low heat 2 minutes. Ladle soup into serving dishes. Top with popcorn and serve immediately.

Maryland Crab Soup   *7 servings*

A Chesapeake Bay specialty known for its spicy vegetable base and chunks of crabmeat. Best made with the backfin meat of the blue crab.

2 tablespoons butter
¼ cup finely chopped onion
¼ cup finely chopped celery
¼ cup finely chopped carrots
½ teaspoon McCormick *Ground Black Pepper*
1 McCormick *Bay Leaf*
⅛ teaspoon McCormick *Ground Red Pepper*

¼ teaspoon McCormick *Ground Mustard*
⅛ teaspoon McCormick *Thyme Leaves*
1½ teaspoons McCormick *Bon Appétit*
1 (28-ounce) can whole tomatoes, chopped, in liquid
2 teaspoons McCormick *Chicken Flavor Base*
4 cups water
1 pound backfin crabmeat

Combine all ingredients, except crabmeat, in large saucepan. Bring to a boil, stirring occasionally. Reduce heat and simmer 15 minutes. Add crabmeat and simmer 5 minutes longer. Remove bay leaf before serving.

Salads

Waldorf Salad *About 8 servings*

Created in 1893 by Oscar of the Waldorf-Astoria Hotel in New York City.

*2 cups cored, diced Red Delicious
    apples
2 cups cored, diced Yellow Delicious
    apples
½ cup chopped celery
½ cup raisins
½ cup chopped walnuts*

*1 cup mayonnaise
2 tablespoons sugar
⅛ teaspoon McCormick Apple Pie
    Spice
⅛ teaspoon McCormick Pure Vanilla
    Extract
Lettuce leaves*

Place apples, celery, raisins, and walnuts in mixing bowl. In small bowl, combine remaining ingredients except lettuce. Mix well. Pour over fruit. Toss gently to mix. Chill. Serve on lettuce leaves.

Supreme Spinach Salad *4 servings*

*½ cup salad oil
¼ cup vinegar
3 tablespoons sugar
¼ cup ketchup
2 teaspoons McCormick Romano
    Cheese Garni®
2 (10-ounce) packages fresh spinach*

*1 (8-ounce) can water chestnuts,
    drained and diced
1 (8-ounce) can bamboo shoots, drained
1 Bermuda onion, sliced and separated
    into rings
4 hard-cooked eggs, peeled and chopped
10 pieces bacon, fried crisp and
    crumbled*

In cruet or small jar, combine oil, vinegar, sugar, ketchup, and Romano Cheese Garni. Shake well. Refrigerate at least 20 minutes to allow flavors to blend. Wash spinach. Tear in bite-size pieces. Drain well. In large salad bowl, combine spinach and remaining ingredients. Pour dressing over all and toss gently. If desired, sprinkle with additional Romano Cheese Garni.

Corn Salad in Pepper Shells *4 servings*

A different, delicious way to serve corn at any time of year.

4 green peppers
⅓ cup salad oil
½ teaspoon McCormick Ground Mustard
½ teaspoon McCormick Ground Black Pepper
⅛ teaspoon McCormick Ground Red Pepper

1 tablespoon McCormick Instant Minced Onion
2 tablespoons vinegar
3 cups whole kernel corn
1 (6-ounce) jar pimiento, cut into 1-inch squares
1 cup thinly sliced celery
1 (8-ounce) can water chestnuts, thinly sliced

Cut tops from green peppers and remove seeds. Cut top edge in petal shape, if desired. Parboil peppers in boiling water 5 minutes. Mix together oil, ground mustard, black and red peppers, minced onion, and vinegar. Combine corn, pimiento, celery, and water chestnuts. Add dressing to corn mixture, tossing to mix well. Fill peppers with corn mixture. Chill, covered.

Potato Salad *About 14 servings*

12 to 15 medium baking potatoes
½ cup thinly sliced celery
½ cup chopped onion
4 hard-cooked eggs, peeled and sliced
1 cup mayonnaise
1 cup sour cream
1 teaspoon McCormick Ground Mustard
¼ teaspoon McCormick Ground Black Pepper

⅛ teaspoon McCormick Ground Red Pepper
1 teaspoon McCormick Whole Coriander Seed
1½ teaspoons McCormick Seasoning Salt
½ pound bacon, cut into 1-inch pieces, cooked and drained

Cook potatoes in skins. Cool slightly, peel, and cut in bite-size cubes. Add celery, onion, and sliced eggs to potato cubes. In small bowl, combine remaining ingredients except bacon. Pour over potato mixture and toss lightly. Chill. Sprinkle with bacon just before serving.

Corn Salad in Pepper Shells

Seafood Salad   *7 servings*

A special salad—great for a luncheon gathering. Must do ahead.

1 cup dry white wine
1 cup water
1 pound sea scallops
1 pound shrimp, peeled and deveined
1 pound crabmeat
1 cucumber, peeled, seeded, and
  chopped
¼ cup mayonnaise
¼ cup sour cream
½ teaspoon lemon juice

⅛ teaspoon McCormick *Ground Black*
  Pepper
½ teaspoon McCormick *Bon Appétit*
1 teaspoon McCormick *Parsley Flakes*
½ teaspoon McCormick *Freeze-Dried*
  Chopped Chives
⅛ teaspoon McCormick *Tarragon*
  Leaves
4 avocados

Combine wine and water in medium saucepan. Bring to a boil. Reduce heat. Add scallops and shrimp. Simmer until just cooked through, about 4 minutes. Drain and cool. In large bowl, combine scallops, shrimp, crabmeat, and cucumber. Toss lightly, then set aside. In bowl, combine remaining ingredients except avocados. Mix well. Pour over seafood mixture. Toss lightly until seafood mixture is evenly coated. Cover and refrigerate overnight. Cut avocados in half lengthwise. Remove seed. Spoon seafood salad over each half.

Water Lily Salad   *6 servings*

A fanciful and tasty salad developed by McCormick in 1913.

6 hard-cooked eggs
¼ teaspoon McCormick *Ground*
  Mustard
½ teaspoon McCormick *Seasoning Salt*
⅛ teaspoon McCormick *Ground Black*
  Pepper

¼ teaspoon McCormick *Dill Weed*
¼ cup mayonnaise
1 head lettuce
1 large white onion, peeled and sliced
1 green pepper, cut into thin strips

Shell eggs and cut in half crosswise. Remove yolks and mash. Mix yolks with mustard, seasoning salt, pepper, dill, and mayonnaise. Fill egg white halves with this mixture. Arrange lettuce on 6 individual salad plates. Cut onion slices in half and separate into strips. Place 2 egg halves in center of lettuce and arrange green pepper and onion strips around them. If desired, serve with mayonnaise on the side.

Note: *Stuffed egg halves can be made a day ahead.*

Main Dishes

Meta

Lamb Chops with Horseradish-Pecan Sauce *6 servings, 1 cup sauce*

Lamb Chops

6 slices bacon
6 boneless lamb loin chops,
  cut 1½ inches thick
1 tablespoon olive oil
1 tablespoon soy sauce
1 tablespoon lemon juice
⅛ teaspoon McCormick *Instant Garlic*
  Powder
⅛ teaspoon McCormick *Instant Onion*
  Powder

Horseradish-Pecan Sauce

1 tablespoon olive oil
1 tablespoon flour
⅛ teaspoon McCormick *Ground White*
  Pepper
1 teaspoon McCormick *Bon Appétit*
⅛ teaspoon McCormick *Instant Minced*
  Garlic
1 cup half-and-half
1 tablespoon prepared horseradish
¼ cup chopped pecans

Preheat broiler. Cook bacon over low heat until cooked but not crisp. Shape lamb chops into rounds. Wrap each chop with 1 piece bacon; secure with wooden toothpick. Place lamb chops on broiler pan. Combine oil, soy sauce, lemon juice, and garlic and onion powders. Brush chops with mixture. Broil 4 inches from heat 10 minutes, or until desired doneness. Turn chops once and brush occasionally during cooking time. Make Horseradish-Pecan Sauce as follows and serve with lamb chops.

Horseradish-Pecan Sauce: Combine olive oil and flour in small saucepan. Add white pepper, Bon Appétit, and minced garlic. Heat until bubbly. Gradually add half-and-half, stirring constantly. Add horseradish and pecans. Cook over medium heat, stirring constantly, until mixture thickens.

Berlin Steaks *5 servings*

2 tablespoons fine dry, unseasoned
    bread crumbs
1 egg, beaten
1/4 teaspoon McCormick *Ground Black
    Pepper*
1/2 teaspoon McCormick *Seasoning Salt*
1 teaspoon McCormick *Instant Minced
    Onion*

1/2 teaspoon McCormick *Parsley Flakes*
1 pound ground beef
1 (.87-ounce) package McCormick
    Brown Gravy Mix
1/4 teaspoon McCormick *Marjoram
    Leaves*
2 tablespoons dry wine (red or white)

Mix together bread crumbs, egg, pepper, seasoning salt, minced onion, and parsley. Gently mix with ground beef. Shape into 5 patties; flatten slightly. In large skillet, brown patties on each side over medium heat. Drain excess fat. Prepare gravy following package directions. Add marjoram and dry wine. Pour gravy over patties in skillet. Cook, covered, over low heat 5 minutes.

Hot and Cold Veal Salad *4 servings, 1 cup sauce*

1/2 pound veal sweetbreads
1/2 pound thin veal cutlets
    cut in 2 × 2 × 1/4-inch pieces
1/2 cup butter
1 tablespoon flour
1/2 cup malt vinegar
2/3 cup water
1/4 teaspoon McCormick *Ground
    Mustard*

1/4 teaspoon McCormick *Paprika*
1/8 teaspoon McCormick *Thyme Leaves*
1/8 teaspoon McCormick *Tarragon
    Leaves*
1/4 teaspoon McCormick *Ground Black
    Pepper*
1/4 teaspoon McCormick *Instant Minced
    Onion*
Salad Greens

Parboil sweetbreads; cool. Remove membrane and cut meat in small pieces, about 2 × 2 × 1/2-inches. Sauté veal and sweetbreads in butter until lightly browned. Remove meat and keep warm. Sprinkle flour over butter in skillet. Stir and cook over low heat 1 minute. Add remaining ingredients except salad greens. Cook, stirring and scraping pan, 1 minute. Pour into heatproof bowl and keep warm. Arrange salad greens on 4 individual plates. Place alternating slices of veal and sweetbreads over greens. Pour 1/4 cup of sauce over meat. Serve immediately.

Hot and Cold Veal Salad

Bavarian Casserole   *4 to 6 servings*

A hearty casserole—wonderful served with hot bread.

2 tablespoons butter
1½ pounds pork, shoulder or loin, cut into 1-inch cubes
2 onions, thinly sliced
1 red bell pepper, cut into small strips
1 (16-ounce) can sauerkraut
2 cups water

2 teaspoons McCormick *Beef Flavor Base*
½ teaspoon McCormick *Seasoning Salt*
1 tablespoon McCormick *Paprika*
1 tablespoon McCormick *Caraway Seed*
1 cup sour cream

Melt butter in large skillet. Sauté meat, onions, and bell pepper 3 minutes over medium heat. Cook sauerkraut with water and beef flavor base 30 minutes. Preheat oven to 350°F. Add remaining ingredients to sauerkraut. Place sauerkraut mixture in 2-quart casserole. Add meat mixture. Stir, if desired. Bake, covered, 30 minutes.

Veal Marsala   *6 servings, 2 pieces each*

¼ cup butter
2 cups sliced mushrooms
1½ pounds veal cutlets, cut ¼-inch thick
2 slices bacon, chopped
¼ cup flour
½ teaspoon McCormick *Instant Garlic Powder*
¼ teaspoon McCormick *Ground Black Pepper*
½ teaspoon McCormick *Seasoning Salt*

¼ cup cold water
1 teaspoon cornstarch
½ cup dry Marsala wine
¼ teaspoon McCormick *Instant Onion Powder*
½ teaspoon McCormick *Marjoram Leaves*
¼ teaspoon McCormick *Basil Leaves*
¼ teaspoon McCormick *Bon Appétit*

In large skillet, melt 1 tablespoon of butter. Sauté mushrooms in hot butter. Remove from skillet and set aside. Cut veal in 12 serving-size pieces. Place bacon in same skillet and cook over low heat until cooked but not crisp. Add 2 tablespoons butter to skillet. Combine flour, garlic powder, pepper, and seasoning salt. Dust veal with flour mixture and sauté, a few pieces at a time, over medium heat 2 minutes on each side. Add remaining butter to skillet when needed. Place veal on serving platter and keep warm. Slowly stir water into cornstarch. Add wine and remaining ingredients. Pour liquid into skillet along with mushrooms. Cook, stirring, over low heat until mixture begins to boil. Pour over veal.

Note: *May use boneless, skinless chicken breasts, pounded to ¼ inch thickness, in place of veal cutlets.*

Zesty Chili Con Carne *4 to 6 servings*

1 pound stew beef, cut into ¹/₂- to ³/₄-inch cubes
1 tablespoon salad oil
2¹/₂ cups water
1 (6-ounce) can tomato paste
2 teaspoons vinegar
3 tablespoons McCormick *Chili Powder*
¹/₈ teaspoon McCormick *Ground Red Pepper*
1¹/₂ teaspoons McCormick *Oregano Leaves*
1¹/₂ teaspoons salt
¹/₈ teaspoon McCormick *Instant Minced Garlic*
¹/₄ teaspoon McCormick *Ground Cumin*
¹/₄ cup McCormick *Instant Chopped Onions*
2 tablespoons McCormick *Green Bell Pepper Flakes*
2 (15¹/₂-ounce) cans kidney beans, drained

In large skillet, brown beef, in hot oil, on all sides. Drain excess fat. Add all remaining ingredients except kidney beans. Cover and simmer 45 minutes. Add beans. Cover and simmer 20 minutes longer.

Microwave Directions: *4 to 5 servings*
Omit oil; substitute 1½ cups water for 2½ cups water. Cut stew beef in ¼ to ½-inch chunks. In 3-quart microwavable casserole dish, combine beef and 1½ cups water. Cook, covered, on medium 8 to 10 minutes, rotating twice. Add remaining ingredients except beans. Cook, covered, on low 20 minutes, rotating and stirring occasionally. Add beans. Cook covered, on low 5 minutes, stirring once. Remove from microwave and let stand, covered, 5 minutes.

Barbecued Country Ribs *About 8 servings*

Spicy country ribs, cooked outdoors.

¹/₂ cup red wine vinegar
¹/₄ cup salad oil
¹/₂ cup tomato sauce
1 tablespoon McCormick *Chili Powder*
2 teaspoons McCormick *Seasoning Salt*
1 teaspoon McCormick *Celery Seed*
2 teaspoons McCormick *Salad Supreme®*
1 teaspoon McCormick *Lemon & Pepper Seasoning Salt*
¹/₂ teaspoon McCormick *Ground Cumin*
5 pounds country-style pork spareribs

Combine all ingredients except spareribs and mix well. Cut spareribs in large serving pieces and place in plastic bag. Add the oil-vinegar mixture and close bag. Chill 2 hours or longer, turning bag occasionally so marinade covers the meat. When ready to cook, drain. Grill slowly about 8 inches from coals, 40 minutes or until well done, turning and basting every 5 to 8 minutes with fresh marinade.

Poultry

Pineapple Brunch Bake   *9 or 10 servings*

2 whole fresh pineapples
18 to 20 slices cooked turkey breast
2 tablespoons butter
2 tablespoons flour
½ teaspoon McCormick *Bon Appétit*
¼ teaspoon McCormick *Ground White Pepper*

Dash McCormick *Ground Allspice*
Dash McCormick *Ground Cardamom*
½ teaspoon McCormick *Instant Minced Onion*
1 McCormick *Bay Leaf*
1 cup milk
1 cup shredded Cheddar cheese

Cut tops from pineapples. Set tops aside. Peel and slice each pineapple in 9 or 10 slices. Remove core from slices. In baking pan, arrange alternating slices of turkey and pineapple in 2 groups, overlapping slices to resemble the shape of 2 pineapples. Preheat oven to 350°F. Melt butter. Stir in flour, Bon Appétit, pepper, allspice, cardamom, and minced onion. Cook, stirring, over low heat 2 to 3 minutes. Add bay leaf. Gradually stir in milk. Gradually add shredded cheese, stirring until cheese melts. Remove bay leaf. Spoon sauce over both pineapples. Bake 15 minutes. If desired, broil until top of sauce is lightly browned. Using 2 large spatulas, transfer pineapples to serving platter. Garnish with pineapple tops.

Turkey with Fruit Stuffing   *12 servings*

A refreshing change and an excellent buffet dish.

2 boneless turkey breast halves
1 (10-ounce) package pitted dates
1 (16-ounce) package dried apricot halves
1 cup walnut pieces
2 cups water
½ teaspoon McCormick *Ground Cinnamon*

¼ teaspoon McCormick *Ground Black Pepper*
¼ teaspoon McCormick *Ground Ginger*
¼ teaspoon McCormick *Ground Nutmeg*
¼ teaspoon McCormick *Ground Cloves*

Cut 3 parallel, lengthwise, 1-inch deep slits in each turkey breast half. Place halves flat in buttered roasting pan. Cut dates in thirds. Cut apricot halves in quarters. Combine dates, apricots, and remaining ingredients in saucepan. Heat, stirring constantly. Simmer 2 minutes, stirring. Cool slightly. Preheat oven to 325°F. Fill slits in turkey with fruit mixture. Bake 2 hours. Cut each breast half in 6 slices.

Turkey with Fruit Stuffing

Sesame Fried Chicken   *About 8 servings*

Good hot, or cold for picnics.

12 pieces broiler-fryer chicken
2 eggs
¼ cup water
¾ cup flour
½ teaspoon McCormick *Turmeric*
1 teaspoon salt

½ teaspoon McCormick *Instant Onion Powder*
¼ teaspoon McCormick *Ground White Pepper*
½ cup McCormick *Sesame Seed, lightly toasted*
Oil for frying

Wash chicken; pat dry. Beat eggs with water. Combine flour, turmeric, salt, onion powder, pepper, and sesame seed; mix well. Roll chicken in flour mixture, dip in egg, and roll in flour mixture again. Fry in hot oil (350°F) until well browned, 30 to 35 minutes. Drain on paper towels.

Note: *To toast sesame seed, spread in shallow baking pan and heat in 350°F oven 10 minutes, or until lightly browned.*

Drunken Chicken   *4 servings*

Chicken in a rich rum sauce.

4 boneless, skinless chicken breast halves
¼ cup light rum
¼ teaspoon McCormick *Ground Nutmeg*
1 tablespoon soy sauce
1 tablespoon lime juice
1 tablespoon brown sugar

¾ teaspoon McCormick *Bon Appétit*
¼ teaspoon McCormick *Crushed Red Pepper*
⅛ teaspoon McCormick *Ground Ginger*
2 tablespoons butter
2 cups sliced mushrooms
1 cup sour cream

Pound chicken breasts to ½-inch thickness. Pierce several times, using tines of a fork. Place in single layer in shallow glass dish. Set aside. Combine rum, nutmeg, soy sauce, lime juice, brown sugar, Bon Appétit, red pepper, and ginger; mix well. Pour liquid over chicken. Marinate at room temperature 30 minutes, turning once. Melt butter in skillet over medium heat. Reserving marinade, remove chicken and sauté in butter. Remove chicken from pan and keep warm. Sauté mushrooms. Reduce heat and add marinade. Gradually add sour cream, stirring until well blended. Cook, covered, over low heat 5 minutes. Serve sauce over chicken breasts. Sprinkle with additional nutmeg, if desired.

Drunken Chicken

Drumsticks with Cream Gravy

6 servings, 1¹/₃ cups gravy

¹/₂ cup flour
1 teaspoon salt
¹/₂ teaspoon McCormick *Ground Black Pepper*
¹/₂ teaspoon McCormick *Instant Garlic Powder*
¹/₂ teaspoon McCormick *Ground Ginger*
12 broiler-fryer chicken drumsticks

¹/₂ cup butter
¹/₂ cup hot water
¹/₂ teaspoon McCormick *Chicken Flavor Base*
¹/₂ teaspoon McCormick *Lemon & Pepper Seasoning Salt*
¹/₂ teaspoon McCormick *Sage Leaves*
1 cup light cream

In plastic bag, mix flour, salt, pepper, garlic powder, and ginger. Add drumsticks, a few at a time, and shake to coat well. Repeat until all drumsticks are coated with seasoned flour. Melt butter in large heavy skillet. Brown drumsticks on all sides slowly and evenly over low heat. Transfer drumsticks to shallow baking pan. Pre-heat oven to 350°F. Pour butter from skillet over chicken, leaving brown drippings in skillet. Bake drumsticks 50 minutes. Combine water, chicken flavor base, lemon & pepper seasoning salt, and sage. Pour into skillet. Bring to a boil, stirring to dissolve drippings. Stir in cream. Bring to a boil again, reduce heat and simmer until slightly thickened. Place drumsticks on serving platter and pour sauce over top.

Hungarian Chicken Paprika

4 to 6 servings

Generous use of paprika gives this special chicken a smooth and mellow flavor.

1 (3-pound) broiler-fryer chicken, cut into pieces
¹/₂ cup flour
1 teaspoon McCormick *Seasoning Salt*
¹/₂ teaspoon McCormick *Ground Thyme*
¹/₄ teaspoon McCormick *Coarse Grind Black Pepper*

¹/₂ cup shortening
2 tablespoons McCormick *Paprika*
¹/₂ teaspoon McCormick *Garlic Salt*
2 cups hot water
2 medium onions
2 tablespoons flour
¹/₂ cup milk

Wash chicken; pat dry. Combine flour, seasoning salt, thyme, and pepper. Coat chicken pieces with flour mixture and fry in hot shortening until lightly browned on all sides. Combine paprika and garlic salt, and sprinkle over chicken. Add hot water and simmer 30 minutes. Slice onions and separate into rings. Place on top of chicken and simmer 30 minutes longer. Remove chicken to serving platter and pile onions on top. Blend together flour and milk; add to liquid in pan. Cook until thickened; pour over chicken.

Fish and Seafood

Oyster Stew   *About 16 servings*

A dish that has changed very little since the early days of oystering on the Chesapeake Bay.

1 cup butter
2 quarts oysters, with liquid
½ teaspoon McCormick *Ground Black Pepper*
2½ teaspoons McCormick *Bon Appétit*
1 tablespoon Worcestershire sauce

¼ teaspoon McCormick *Instant Onion Powder*
⅛ teaspoon McCormick *Oregano Leaves*
1 half-gallon milk
1 quart half-and-half or light cream

In 6-quart enamel or stainless steel kettle, melt butter. Add oysters with liquid, pepper, Bon Appétit, Worcestershire sauce, onion powder, and oregano. Simmer 5 minutes, stirring occasionally. Stir in milk and cream. Heat slowly. Do not boil.

Note: This recipe is easily halved or doubled, depending on the number of people to be served.

Maryland Crab Cakes   *4 servings*

A Maryland specialty, best made with the backfin meat of the blue crab.

1 slice white bread, crust removed
1 egg, beaten
1 tablespoon mayonnaise
1 teaspoon McCormick *Parsley Flakes*
½ teaspoon McCormick *Bon Appétit*
½ teaspoon salt
¼ teaspoon McCormick *Ground Mustard*
⅛ teaspoon McCormick *Basil Leaves*

⅛ teaspoon McCormick *Ground Ginger*
⅛ teaspoon McCormick *Ground Black Pepper*
⅛ teaspoon McCormick *Ground Red Pepper*
Dash McCormick *Ground Cloves*
1 pound backfin crabmeat
Oil for frying

Crumble bread into fine crumbs. Mix bread with remaining ingredients, except crabmeat and oil. Let stand until bread dissolves. Combine crabmeat with bread mixture; toss gently. Shape into 8 cakes. Fry in hot oil (375°F) in skillet or deep-fat fryer 4 minutes, or until golden brown, or brush with melted butter and broil.

Note: You may substitute 1 teaspoon McCormick *Chesapeake Bay Style Seafood Seasoning for the 9 seasonings listed above.*

Lobster with Vanilla Sauce   *3 to 4 servings*

1 cup butter
½ teaspoon lemon juice

¼ teaspoon McCormick *Pure Vanilla
   Extract*
3 or 4 hot steamed lobsters

Melt butter in small saucepan. Remove from heat; cool slightly. Carefully pour off clear portion of butter into a small mixing bowl. Add lemon juice and vanilla. Mix well. Serve sauce hot with steamed lobster.

Sole Mousse
with Shrimp Sauce   *6 servings, 3 cups sauce*

Sole Mousse
1 pound filet of sole, cut in small pieces
2 cups whipping cream
4 eggs
⅔ cup milk
1 tablespoon McCormick *Parsley Flakes*
1½ teaspoons salt
¼ teaspoon McCormick *Ground Savory*
⅛ teaspoon McCormick *Ground White
   Pepper*
Dash McCormick *Ground Red Pepper*
1 tablespoon butter
1 tablespoon fine dry, unseasoned bread
   crumbs
¼ teaspoon McCormick *Dill Weed*

Shrimp Sauce
¼ cup butter
3 tablespoons flour
1½ cups half-and-half
½ teaspoon salt
½ teaspoon McCormick *Instant Onion
   Powder*
3 tablespoons dry sherry
1 tablespoon lemon juice
2 teaspoons McCormick *Parsley Flakes*
2 cups cooked shrimp, shelled and
   deveined

Place about ½ cup cream in blender; add ¼ of the fish; blend at medium speed until smooth. Add 1 egg, scrape sides; blend again until smooth. Mixture will become very thick. Pour into bowl, and repeat until all of the fish is blended with all of the cream. Stir milk, parsley flakes, salt, savory, and peppers into fish mixture, blending well. Preheat oven to 350°F. Spread butter into 6-cup ring mold. Combine bread crumbs and dill weed; sprinkle over bottom and sides of mold. Spoon fish mixture into mold; level top. Set in hot water. Bake 45 minutes, or until top is lightly browned and knife inserted into center comes out clean. Let stand 15 minutes then unmold. Make Shrimp Sauce as follows and serve with mousse.

Shrimp Sauce: Melt butter in saucepan. Stir in flour. Add half-and-half, salt, and onion powder. Cook, stirring, until sauce boils and thickens. Stir in sherry, lemon juice, and parsley flakes. Add shrimp and heat through.

Lobster with Vanilla Sauce

Pasta and Rice

Oriental Rice *7 servings*

3 tablespoons butter
Dash McCormick *Ground Cloves*
¼ teaspoon McCormick *Ground Cinnamon*
¼ teaspoon McCormick *Ground Cardamom*
⅛ teaspoon McCormick *Ground Allspice*
⅛ teaspoon McCormick *Saffron, crushed*
⅛ teaspoon McCormick *Ground Black Pepper*
2 teaspoons McCormick *Garlic Salt*
½ teaspoon McCormick *Bon Appétit*
2 tablespoons McCormick *Instant Minced Onion*
1 cup long grain rice
3 cups boiling water
½ cup raisins
½ cup toasted slivered almonds

Melt butter in saucepan. Add seasonings and rice; mix well. Add boiling water, cover, and simmer 25 minutes. Add raisins. Let stand, covered, 5 minutes. Sprinkle with almonds.

▼▲▼

Lasagna *6 servings*

1 pound ground beef
1 (1½-ounce) package McCormick *Spaghetti Sauce Mix*
1 (6-ounce) can tomato paste
1⅓ cups water
1 tablespoon butter
1 teaspoon McCormick *Oregano Leaves*
½ pound lasagna noodles
2 cups cottage or ricotta cheese
½ pound mozzarella cheese slices

Brown ground beef in saucepan. Drain excess fat. Add spaghetti sauce mix, tomato paste, water, butter, and oregano. Mix well. Bring to a boil. Reduce heat, cover, and simmer 10 minutes. Cook noodles, following package directions. Rinse in cold water, drain, and separate. Preheat oven to 350°F. In buttered 11¾ × 7½ × 1¾-inch baking dish, layer noodles, meat sauce, cottage cheese, and mozzarella cheese slices, in that order; repeat layers. Bake 25 minutes, or until bubbly.

Spaghetti with Meatballs (page 38)

Spaghetti with Meatballs *4 servings, 2½ cups sauce*

1 (1½-ounce) package McCormick
  Spaghetti Sauce Mix
1 (6-ounce) can tomato paste
2¼ cups water
1 tablespoon butter
½ teaspoon McCormick *Italian
  Seasoning*
½ teaspoon McCormick *Instant Minced
  Onion*
1 pound ground beef

1 teaspoon McCormick *Seasoning Salt*
¼ teaspoon McCormick *Ground Black
  Pepper*
¼ teaspoon McCormick *Instant Onion
  Powder*
2 tablespoons vegetable oil
½ teaspoon McCormick *Beef Flavor
  Base*
¼ cup hot tap water
½ pound spaghetti

In saucepan, combine spaghetti sauce mix, tomato paste, water, butter, Italian seasoning, and minced onion. Bring to a boil. Reduce heat, cover, and simmer 20 minutes. Combine beef, seasoning salt, black pepper, and onion powder. Mix well. Shape into 8 balls (1½ inches in diameter). Brown in hot oil. Dissolve beef flavor base in water. Pour over meatballs. Cover and simmer 20 minutes. Cook spaghetti, following package directions. Serve sauce over spaghetti. Top with meatballs. (See photo, page 37.)

Pasta Primavera *4 to 5 servings*

A new-wave Italian dish with a rich, creamy sauce.

6 ounces fettucine (yields 3 cups cooked)
¼ cup butter
1 tablespoon flour
½ teaspoon McCormick *Instant Garlic
  Powder*
¼ teaspoon McCormick *Instant Onion
  Powder*
¼ teaspoon McCormick *Parsley Flakes*
Dash McCormick *Ground Nutmeg*
⅛ teaspoon McCormick *Ground White
  Pepper*

¼ teaspoon McCormick *Bon Appétit*
¾ cup whipping cream
½ cup shredded Havarti cheese
*½ cup carrots,
  cut in ¼ × ¼ × 1-inch sticks*
1 cup broccoli florets
*1 cup Italian green beans, cut in
  1-inch pieces*
*½ cup Italian plum tomatoes, peeled
  and coarsely chopped*

Cook fettucine, according to package directions, while preparing sauce. Melt butter in 2-quart saucepan. Gradually stir in flour and seasonings. Cook 1 minute, stirring with wire whisk. Gradually add cream and shredded cheese. Stir until cheese melts. Drain fettucine and put in large, warmed bowl. Add vegetables and sauce. Toss and serve immediately.

Pasta Primavera

Vegetables

Green Bean Casserole *6 servings*

2 (9-ounce) packages frozen French-cut
   green beans
1 (10¾-ounce) can condensed cream of
   mushroom soup
¼ cup milk
¼ teaspoon McCormick *Seasoning Salt*

⅛ teaspoon McCormick *Ground Black
   Pepper*
1 tablespoon dry sherry
2 tablespoons chopped pimiento,
   drained
1 (2.8-ounce) can French-fried onions

Preheat oven to 350°F. Cook green beans, following package directions. Drain. In 1½-quart casserole, combine green beans, soup, milk, seasoning salt, pepper, sherry, and pimiento. Add half of the onions. Mix well. Bake, uncovered, 20 minutes. Top with remaining onions and bake 5 minutes longer.

Note: *You may substitute 3 cups fresh cut green beans, cooked, or 2 (16-ounce) cans green beans, drained, for frozen green beans.*

Maryland Fried Tomatoes *6 servings*

A taste of the old South, this is an excellent use for end-of-the-season tomatoes.

4 large, slightly underripe tomatoes
¼ cup fine dry, unseasoned bread
   crumbs
½ cup flour
1 teaspoon McCormick *Seasoning Salt*
¼ teaspoon McCormick *Thyme Leaves*

½ teaspoon McCormick *Ground Black
   Pepper*
⅛ teaspoon McCormick *Ground Red
   Pepper*
1 egg, beaten with 1 tablespoon water
Butter

Wash tomatoes and remove stems. Cut each tomato in 3 thick slices. Combine bread crumbs with flour, seasoning salt, thyme, pepper, and red pepper. Mix well. Dip tomato slices in egg mixture, then roll in crumb mixture. Sauté in melted butter over medium heat, turning once, to lightly brown both sides. Serve hot.

Caramel Sweet Potatoes *8 servings*

4 large sweet potatoes
½ cup water
⅓ cup butter
½ cup dark brown sugar
¼ cup chopped walnuts

¾ teaspoon McCormick Pure Vanilla
   Extract
¼ teaspoon McCormick Pumpkin Pie
   Spice
⅛ teaspoon McCormick Lemon Peel
¼ cup dark corn syrup

Wash potatoes. Place in large saucepan or Dutch oven. Cover with water. Bring to a boil. Reduce heat, cover, and simmer until tender, about 25 to 30 minutes. Drain and cool. Peel and quarter potatoes. Preheat oven to 375°F. Place potatoes in buttered 13 × 9 × 2-inch baking dish. Set aside. Combine remaining ingredients in small saucepan. Simmer 5 minutes. Pour sauce over potatoes. Bake, uncovered, 50 minutes, basting with sauce several times.

Note: You can use sauce portion with drained, canned sweet potatoes.

Microwave Directions: *6 cups*
Substitute 4 medium-size sweet potatoes (2½ × 5 inches) for large sweet potatoes and ¼ cup water for ½ cup water. Remaining ingredients use the same measurements. Wash potatoes. Prick potatoes over entire surface, using tines of a fork. Place in circular pattern on microwave floor. Cook, uncovered, on high 12 to 15 minutes, rotating every 4 minutes. Let stand 8 minutes. Peel and quarter. Place in microwavable 9-inch pie plate. Set aside. Combine remaining ingredients in medium microwavable bowl. Cook, uncovered, on high 4 to 6 minutes, stirring twice. Pour sauce over potatoes. Cook, uncovered, on medium 8 to 10 minutes, rotating plate and basting potatoes with sauce several times.

Easy Baked Beans *4 to 6 servings*

1½ teaspoon McCormick Ground
   Ginger
1 teaspoon McCormick Ground
   Mustard
1 teaspoon McCormick Almond Extract
1 tablespoon lemon juice

¼ cup dark brown sugar, packed
½ cup chili sauce
2 tablespoons dry wine (red or white)
1 (18 ounce) jar baked beans
1 medium-size onion

In a 1½ to 2-quart bowl, combine all ingredients, except beans and onion. Mix well. Stir in beans. Preheat oven to 350°F. Pour half the mixture in buttered 1½-quart baking dish. Slice onion and separate into rings and place over beans. Top with remaining beans. Cover and bake 1 hour.

Cucumber Stir-Fry   *4 servings*

A hot cucumber salad—an excellent use for winter cucumbers.

4 slices bacon
1 small yellow onion, peeled and cut in
  ¹/₈-inch slices
2 cucumbers, peeled, seeded, and cut in
  julienne strips
1 medium red pepper, seeded and cut in
  small, thin strips
¹/₈ teaspoon McCormick Ground White
  Pepper

¹/₄ teaspoon McCormick Celery Seed
¹/₄ teaspoon McCormick Seasoning Salt
¹/₄ teaspoon McCormick Parsley Flakes
¹/₄ teaspoon sugar
3 tablespoons water
2 tablespoons red wine vinegar
¹/₂ teaspoon cornstarch

Fry bacon. Drain, reserving 2 tablespoons bacon fat. Set aside. Separate onion slices into rings. Heat bacon fat in skillet over medium-high heat. Add cucumbers, red peppers, and onion rings. Stir-fry 3 minutes. Remove vegetables from skillet. Combine remaining ingredients. Mix well. Add to skillet, stirring constantly, until mixture thickens. Add vegetables and heat through. Arrange cucumbers, peppers, and onion rings on 4 individual plates. Garnish with crumbled bacon.

Creamed Asparagus   *4 to 6 servings*

A seasonal favorite.

2 pounds fresh asparagus
3 tablespoons butter
2 tablespoons flour
2 teaspoons McCormick Bon Appétit
¹/₈ teaspoon McCormick Ground
  Coriander

¹/₄ teaspoon McCormick Ground White
  Pepper
¹/₈ teaspoon McCormick Italian
  Seasoning
1 cup whipping cream
1 cup milk

Wash asparagus. Peel thick part of stems. Steam asparagus until tender. Cool slightly, then cut in 2-inch pieces. Melt butter in saucepan. Stir in flour, Bon Appétit, coriander, white pepper, and Italian seasoning. Cook, stirring constantly, 2 to 3 minutes. Gradually stir in whipping cream and milk. Cook, stirring, until sauce thickens slightly. Add asparagus pieces. Cook 1 minute.

Breads

Black Bread   *2 loaves*

Fun for collectors of special bread recipes.

½ cup cornmeal
2 cups water
¼ cup butter, cut in pieces
1 ounce unsweetened chocolate
½ cup dark molasses
1½ teaspoons salt

2 tablespoons McCormick *Caraway Seed*
2 teaspoons instant coffee
¼ cup lukewarm water
1 (¼-ounce) package active dry yeast
5½ cups flour

In saucepan, combine cornmeal and water. Cook, stirring, over medium heat until mixture comes to a boil. Simmer 1 minute. Remove from heat. Add butter, chocolate, molasses, salt, caraway seed, and instant coffee. Mix well. Cool to lukewarm. Combine lukewarm water and yeast. Let stand 5 minutes. Stir into cornmeal mixture. Beat in 4½ cups flour, ½ cup at a time. Place dough on well-floured surface and knead in remaining flour. Continue kneading until dough is smooth and elastic, about 5 minutes. Butter inside of large bowl. Place dough in bowl. Turn dough until entire surface is lightly buttered. Cover with towel. Set in warm, draft-free place and let rise 1½ hours, or until double in size. Punch dough down. Knead 2 minutes on floured surface. Divide dough in half and shape each half into small loaf. Place each loaf in buttered 2¼ × 3½ × 7½-inch loaf pan. Cover with towel and let rise 40 minutes. Preheat oven to 350°F. Bake 1 hour, or until loaves shrink away from sides of pan. Cool on wire racks.

Spoonbread   *6 to 8 servings*

A moist, fluffy cornbread, Southern cousin to a soufflé.

¾ cup yellow cornmeal
2¼ cups milk
1 (17-ounce) can whole kernel corn
½ cup melted butter
1 cup flour
1 teaspoon McCormick Seasoning Salt

¼ teaspoon McCormick Thyme Leaves
¼ teaspoon McCormick Ground Red
  Pepper
2 tablespoons sugar
2 teaspoons baking powder
4 eggs, beaten

In stainless steel bowl over boiling water, combine cornmeal and milk. Stir until smooth. Cook, stirring occasionally, 10 minutes. Stir in corn and melted butter. Preheat oven to 350°F. Mix flour with seasoning salt, thyme, red pepper, sugar, and baking powder. Stir into corn mixture. Stir in beaten eggs. Pour into greased 9-inch square baking pan or a 9-inch cast iron skillet. Bake 45 to 50 minutes. Serve hot in pan. Use a large spoon to scoop out servings.

Pain Perdu Roanoke (Lost Bread)   *12 servings*

Thick, deep-fried French toast made with cornbread, crusty on the outside, moist on the inside.

1 (10-ounce) package cornbread mix
1 (12-ounce) can whole kernel corn
⅛ teaspoon McCormick Ground Red
  Pepper
¼ teaspoon McCormick Ground Savory
3 eggs
1 cup milk
1 tablespoon sugar

¼ teaspoon McCormick Ground
  Nutmeg
½ teaspoon McCormick Pure Vanilla
  Extract
Oil for frying
Confectioners' sugar
Maple syrup

Preheat oven to 400°F. Prepare cornbread batter, following package directions. Add corn, red pepper, and savory. Pour into greased 8 × 4 × 3-inch loaf pan. Bake 30 minutes. Remove from pan. Cool. Cut in 6 thick slices. Cut each slice in half diagonally to make 12 triangular pieces. Beat eggs. Add milk, sugar, nutmeg, and vanilla. Mix well. Place oil, 2 inches deep, in skillet and heat to 350°F. Soak cornbread in egg mixture. Carefully remove each piece and lower into hot fat. Fry 4 to 5 minutes, turning once. Use a slotted spoon to lift bread out of oil. Drain on absorbent paper. Sprinkle with confectioners' sugar and serve with maple syrup.

Pain Perdu Roanoke

Cakes and Cookies

Ginger Bites *12½ dozen cookies*

½ cup butter, softened
½ cup sugar
½ cup molasses
2 eggs
1 teaspoon baking soda

1 teaspoon McCormick *Ground Ginger*
½ teaspoon McCormick *Cinnamon*
3¼ cups flour
1 teaspoon McCormick *Pure Vanilla Extract*

Preheat oven to 350°F. Cream butter with sugar. Beat in molasses and eggs. Combine baking soda, ginger, cinnamon, and flour. Add flour mixture gradually to creamed mixture, mixing well. Stir in vanilla extract. On board dusted with confectioners' sugar, roll out small amount of dough at a time, to ⅛ inch thickness. Cut out cookies using very small (1 to 1¼-inch) cutters, or use a knife to cut 1-inch squares. Bake on ungreased cookie sheets 5 minutes. Cool on wire racks. (See photo, page 51.)

Microwave Truffles *50 truffles*

24 ounces semisweet chocolate pieces
2 tablespoons butter
2 tablespoons sour cream
½ teaspoon McCormick *Imitation Brandy Extract*
½ teaspoon McCormick *Imitation Rum Extract*

½ teaspoon McCormick *Pure Vanilla Extract*
Unsweetened cocoa powder
Flaked coconut
Finely chopped pecans

Place chocolate, butter, and sour cream in 3-quart microwavable container. Cover and cook in microwave oven at full power 2 minutes. Stir thoroughly. Cook 1 minute longer. Stir. Divide mixture into 3 portions. Add brandy extract to one portion, rum extract to the second portion, and vanilla extract to the third portion. Mix each portion well. Shape into 1-inch balls and roll in cocoa, coconut, or chopped pecans. Store in airtight container. (See photo, page 51.)

Praline Lace Cookies *4½ dozen cookies*

¼ cup butter
¼ cup light corn syrup
¼ cup light brown sugar
½ cup plus 2 tablespoons flour, sifted before measuring
¼ teaspoon baking powder

⅛ teaspoon McCormick Ground Nutmeg
¼ teaspoon McCormick Ground Cinnamon
⅓ cup McCormick Sesame Seed, lightly toasted
54 pecan halves

Preheat oven to 325°F. Melt butter, corn syrup, and brown sugar in top of double boiler over simmering water. Sift together flour, baking powder, nutmeg, and cinnamon. Stir into butter mixture. Add sesame seed. Stir to blend. Drop by ½ teaspoonfuls, 3 inches apart, on greased baking sheet. Center a pecan half on each cookie. Bake 8 minutes. Cool on baking sheet about 2 minutes. Remove with thin spatula. Finish cooling on flat surface.

Note: To toast sesame seed, spread in shallow baking pan and heat in 350°F oven 10 minutes, or until lightly browned.

———— ▼▲▼ ————

Original Style Chocolate Chip Cookies *4½ dozen cookies*

In the style of the all-time American favorite invented at the Toll House Inn.

1 cup butter, softened
½ cup sugar
1 cup brown sugar
1 teaspoon McCormick Pure Vanilla Extract
2 eggs
2¼ cups flour, sifted before measuring

⅛ teaspoon McCormick Ground Cinnamon
1 teaspoon baking soda
1 teaspoon salt
1 cup chopped walnuts
2 (4-ounce) packages German's sweet chocolate, cut into ¾-inch squares

Preheat oven to 350°F. In large bowl, combine butter, sugars, and vanilla. Beat until creamy. Add eggs. Sift together flour, cinnamon, baking soda, and salt. Gradually add dry ingredients to butter mixture. Mix well. Stir in walnuts and chocolate squares. Drop by rounded teaspoonfuls onto greased cookie sheets. Bake 8 to 10 minutes, or until golden brown. Cool on wire rack.

Holiday Cookies

1 cup butter	2½ cups sifted flour
1 cup sugar	¼ teaspoon McCormick *Mace*
1 teaspoon McCormick *Pure Vanilla Extract*	¾ cup finely chopped green and red cherries
½ teaspoon McCormick *Imitation Rum Extract*	½ cup finely chopped pecans
	¾ cup flaked coconut

Cream together butter and sugar. Stir in vanilla and rum extracts. Stir in flour, mace, cherries, and nuts. Chill dough. Shape into rolls 1 inch in diameter. Roll in coconut. Wrap in wax paper and chill. Dough may be frozen at this stage and baked as needed. Preheat oven to 375°F. Slice dough ¼ inch thick. Place on ungreased cookie sheets. Bake 5 to 7 minutes, or until edges are golden.

Note: Use either candied or maraschino cherries. If maraschino cherries are used, drain chopped cherries well on paper towels.

Depression Cake   *8 servings*

So-named because it was developed during hard times when rich ingredients were unavailable.

Cake

2 cups flour	1 cup mayonnaise
1 cup sugar	1 cup water
¼ cup unsweetened cocoa powder	2 teaspoons McCormick *Pure Vanilla Extract*
1 teaspoon baking powder	½ cup raisins
½ teaspoon baking soda	½ cup chopped walnuts
1 teaspoon McCormick *Ground Cinnamon*	**Glaze**
½ teaspoon McCormick *Ground Cloves*	1 cup confectioners' sugar
½ teaspoon McCormick *Ground Nutmeg*	2 tablespoons water
	½ teaspoon McCormick *Imitation Rum Extract*

Preheat oven to 350°F. Stir together flour, sugar, cocoa powder, baking powder, baking soda, cinnamon, cloves, and nutmeg. Set aside. Combine mayonnaise, water, and vanilla. Add mayonnaise mixture to dry ingredients. Beat until blended, about 2 minutes. Fold in raisins and walnuts. Pour into greased and floured 9 × 9 × 2-inch baking pan. Bake 30 to 35 minutes, or until cake tests done. Cool on wire rack 5 minutes. Remove cake from pan. Cool. Mix glaze ingredients together well. Spread glaze evenly over cake.

Holiday Cookies, Ginger Bites (page 48), Microwave Truffles (page 48)

Cinnamon Chocolate Cake

A rich and velvety dark chocolate cake.

¾ cup butter
2¼ cups sugar
2 teaspoons McCormick *Pure Vanilla*
Extract
1 teaspoon McCormick *Ground*
Cinnamon
6 eggs

4 (1-ounce) squares unsweetened baking
chocolate, melted
3 cups cake flour, sifted before
measuring
2 teaspoons baking soda
1 teaspoon salt
1½ cups ice water
Fudge Frosting (recipe below)

Cream together butter, sugar, vanilla, and cinnamon until smooth and fluffy. Add eggs and beat until light and fluffy. Beat in melted chocolate. Sift together cake flour, baking soda, and salt. Add ⅓ of the dry ingredients to the chocolate mixture. Stir in, using wire whisk. Add ¾ cup ice water, stirring until well mixed. Repeat using ⅓ of the dry ingredients and the remaining ice water; stir in remaining dry ingredients. Preheat oven to 350°F. Grease and line three 9-inch round cake pans with wax paper. Divide batter evenly among the pans. Bake 35 to 40 minutes. Do not over bake. Cool 10 minutes in pans. Remove from pans. Place one layer on serving plate. Spread with a small amount of Fudge Frosting. Add second layer and spread with frosting. Add top layer. Spread top and sides with Fudge Frosting.

Note: Cake can also be baked in a 13 × 9 × 3-inch pan. Bake in 350°F oven 1 hour. Frost cake, using ½ recipe for Fudge Frosting. Raspberry preserves or chocolate pudding may be substituted for Fudge Frosting between cake layers.

Fudge Frosting *Frosts one 3-layer cake*

2 (12-ounce) packages semisweet
chocolate chips
1 (14-ounce) can sweetened condensed
milk

½ teaspoon McCormick *Ground*
Cinnamon
1 teaspoon McCormick *Pure Vanilla*
Extract
½ cup coffee liqueur

In stainless steel bowl over boiling water, combine chocolate chips, milk, cinnamon, and vanilla. Cover bowl with foil. Remove pan from heat. Let stand until chocolate melts. Add coffee liqueur and stir until smooth and glossy.

Desserts

Special Pumpkin Pie *8 servings*

Pie
9-inch uncooked pastry pie shell
2 eggs
1 (16-ounce) can pumpkin, about 2 cups
½ cup brown sugar
1 teaspoon McCormick Ground Cinnamon
¼ teaspoon McCormick Ground Nutmeg
¼ teaspoon McCormick Ground Ginger
¼ teaspoon McCormick Ground Cloves
½ teaspoon salt
1 (13-ounce) can evaporated milk

Spiced Pecan Topping
2 tablespoons brown sugar
2 tablespoons butter

⅛ teaspoon McCormick Ground Cinnamon
⅛ teaspoon McCormick Ground Nutmeg
Dash McCormick Ground Cloves
1 cup coarsely chopped pecans

Spiced Whipped Cream
1 cup whipping cream
6 tablespoons confectioners' sugar
¼ teaspoon McCormick Ground Cinnamon
⅛ teaspoon McCormick Ground Nutmeg
⅛ teaspoon McCormick Ground Cloves
1 teaspoon McCormick Pure Vanilla Extract

Preheat oven to 450°F. Line 9-inch pie plate with pastry. Beat eggs until light. Stir in pumpkin. Combine brown sugar with spices and salt. Stir into pumpkin mixture. Gradually stir in evaporated milk. Pour into pastry shell. Bake 15 minutes. Reduce temperature to 350°F and bake 40 minutes longer. Cool. Make Spiced Pecan Topping and Spiced Whipped Cream as follows. Sprinkle with Spiced Pecan Topping and decorate with spoonfuls of Spiced Whipped Cream.

Spiced Pecan Topping: In large heavy skillet, mix together brown sugar, butter, cinnamon, nutmeg, and cloves. Heat, stirring, until sugar begins to melt. Quickly stir in pecans. Stir to coat nuts evenly with sugar. Cool.

Spiced Whipped Cream: Combine whipping cream and confectioners' sugar. Add cinnamon, nutmeg, and cloves. Beat until stiff. Stir in vanilla extract.

Cardinal Punch *8 cups*

A frozen slush, served between courses at White House dinners during McKinley's administration.

1 (48-ounce) bottle cranberry juice cocktail
2 tablespoons lemon juice
2 cups light corn syrup
1 (3-inch) piece McCormick *Cinnamon Stick*

1 (1-inch) piece McCormick *Whole Ginger*
2 McCormick *Whole Cardamom Seeds*
1 McCormick *Bay Leaf*
Fresh mint sprigs

Combine all ingredients in enamel or stainless steel kettle. Heat slowly and warm over low heat 10 minutes. Remove whole spices. Pour liquid into an 11 × 8 × 2-inch roasting pan. Freeze until solid. Remove from freezer. Scratch with tines of a fork until all of the mixture is broken into small flakes. Work quickly and return pan to freezer. To serve, pile frozen slush in sherbet glasses. Garnish with fresh mint. Serve between courses to refresh the palate, or as a refreshing, light dessert.

Australian Pavlova *8 to 10 servings*

An Australian national favorite, simple but spectacular.

4 egg whites, at room temperature
Dash salt
1 cup super-fine sugar
1 teaspoon vinegar
1 teaspoon cornstarch

1½ teaspoons McCormick *Pure Vanilla Extract*
1 pint whipping cream
¾ cup confectioners' sugar
1 pint strawberries
3 kiwi fruit

Preheat oven to 275°F. Beat egg whites with salt. Gradually add sugar, beating until very thick. Beat in vinegar, cornstarch, and ½ teaspoon vanilla extract. Grease a baking sheet and dust heavily with cornstarch. Spoon meringue onto center of baking sheet. Spread with back of spoon to make 9-inch round or oval. Bake 1 hour. Do not brown. Cool in oven with door open. Place meringue on serving plate. Whip cream with confectioners' sugar and remaining 1 teaspoon vanilla until stiff. Chill. Wash and hull strawberries. Peel and slice kiwi fruit. Save 6 whole strawberries and 6 to 8 slices kiwi for garnish. Slice remaining berries. Place sliced berries and kiwi on meringue. Spread about ⅓ of whipped cream over fruit. Using a pastry bag with large star tip, pipe whipped cream to cover sides. Pipe large rosettes of cream around top and bottom. Garnish with reserved fruit. Cut in wedges.

Australian Pavlova

Piña Colada Soufflé   *16 servings*

A spectacular dessert for special dinner parties.

2 envelopes unflavored gelatin
1½ cups canned pineapple juice, chilled
8 eggs, separated
½ teaspoon salt
1 cup sugar
⅛ teaspoon McCormick Ground Mace
⅛ teaspoon McCormick Ground Cardamom

½ teaspoon McCormick Imitation Rum Extract
1 cup whipping cream
2 tablespoons confectioners' sugar
¼ cup dark rum
1 cup cream of coconut
Sweetened whipped cream

Soften gelatin in ½ cup chilled pineapple juice. In top of double boiler, combine egg yolks, salt, ¼ cup of sugar, mace, cardamom, and remaining pineapple juice. Cook over boiling water, stirring constantly, until slightly thickened. Add gelatin mixture and rum extract. Stir until gelatin dissolves. Pour into large bowl. Cool. To prepare 6-cup soufflé dish, fold a 30-inch strip of foil in half lengthwise. Tie foil with string around outside of dish to make a collar standing about 5 inches above rim. Beat egg whites until foamy. Gradually add remaining sugar. Beat until stiff peaks form when beaters are lifted. Whip cream with confectioners' sugar. Add rum and cream of coconut to gelatin mixture. Stir well. Gently fold in egg whites and whipped cream. Pour into prepared soufflé dish. Refrigerate at least 3 hours. Cut string and carefully remove foil collar. Garnish soufflé with sweetened whipped cream. (See photo, page 59.)

▼▲▼

Strawberries with Brie Sauce   *¾ cup sauce*

Contemporary and dramatic in appearance and taste.

4 ounces Brie cheese, crust removed and softened to room temperature
½ cup whipping cream
2 teaspoons sugar
Dash McCormick Ground Cardamom

¼ teaspoon McCormick Pure Vanilla Extract
Dash McCormick Orange Extract
Whole fresh strawberries, chilled

Cut cheese in small pieces. Combine whipping cream, sugar, and cardamom in top of double boiler over simmering water. Heat until sugar dissolves. Add Brie. Stir occasionally until Brie melts. Remove from heat when smooth and creamy. Add extracts. Stir to mix well. Spoon sauce over whole, chilled strawberries.

Note: This must be prepared just before serving.

Baked Maple Custard   *6 servings*

2 cups milk
6 tablespoons maple syrup
1/4 cup finely chopped walnuts
4 eggs
1/3 cup sugar
1/4 teaspoon salt

3/4 teaspoon McCormick *Imitation
    Maple Flavor*
1/16 teaspoon McCormick *Ground
    Nutmeg*
1/8 teaspoon McCormick *Ground
    Cinnamon*

Preheat oven to 350°F. Scald milk; set aside. Put 1 tablespoon maple syrup in each of six 6-ounce custard cups. Sprinkle 2 teaspoons walnuts over syrup in each cup. Set aside. In medium bowl, combine eggs, sugar, and salt. Beat well. Stir in milk, maple flavor, nutmeg, and cinnamon. Blend well. Pour mixture into custard cups, dividing it evenly among the 6 custard cups. Set cups in baking pan. Pour hot water in pan to depth of 1 inch. Bake 40 minutes, or until an inserted knife comes out clean. Remove from oven. Let cool; refrigerate overnight. To serve, loosen custard around edges and invert over serving plate. Shake to loosen custard.

Microwave Directions: *six 6-ounce custards*
Use same ingredients. Pour milk into 1-quart microwavable measuring cup. Cook, uncovered, on medium 5 to 6 minutes or until scalded. Put 1 tablespoon maple syrup in each of six 6-ounce microwavable custard cups. Sprinkle 2 teaspoons walnuts over syrup in each cup. Set aside. In medium bowl, combine remaining ingredients. Beat well. Stir in milk. Blend well. Pour mixture into custard cups, dividing evenly among the 6 custard cups. Arrange cups in circular pattern in microwave. Cook, uncovered, on medium 8 to 10 minutes or until custard is set. Rotate cups occasionally. Remove from microwave. Let cool; refrigerate overnight. To serve, loosen custard around edges and invert over serving plate. Shake to loosen custard.

Lemon Ginger Ice   *3 cups*

2 cups water
1 cup sugar
1 cup lemon juice

1 drop McCormick *Yellow Food Color*
1 drop McCormick *Anise Extract*
4 teaspoons McCormick *Minced
    Crystallized Ginger*

In 2-quart saucepan, bring water and sugar to a boil over medium heat. Stir only until sugar dissolves. Cook mixture 5 minutes. Remove pan from heat. Cool to room temperature. Stir in remaining ingredients. Pour mixture into an ice cube tray without divider. Freeze 4 hours, stirring every 30 minutes, scraping particles from around edges of tray into the middle.

Piña Colada Soufflé (page 56)

Index